HEAVEN

FINDING OUR TRUE HOME

DOUGLAS
CONNELLY

8 STUDIES
FOR INDIVIDUALS
OR GROUPS

ivp

Life

Builder

Study

INTER-VARSITY PRESS
36 Causton Street, London SW1P 4ST, England
Email: ivp@ivpbooks.com
Website: www.ivpbooks.com

Originally published in the United States of America in the LifeGuide® Bible Studies series in 2000 by InterVarsity Press, Downers Grove, Illinois
First published in Great Britain by Scripture Union in 2010
Second edition published in 2015
This edition published in Great Britain by Inter-Varsity Press 2020

British Library Cataloguing-in-Publication Data
A catalogue record for this book is available from the British Library.

ISBN: 978–1–78359–837–3

Printed in Great Britain by Ashford Colour Press Ltd, Gosport, Hampshire

Contents

Getting the Most Out of *Heaven*

Probably no word brings more calm into our lives than the word *heaven*. But when most Christians actually try to describe their future life in heaven, the picture gets pretty fuzzy. To some people heaven looks like perpetual retirement—sitting on a cloud, strumming a harp. Other people think of heaven as an endless church service. We all want to go to this place called "heaven," but we are unsure about what it will really be like. What we need is accurate, reliable information about heaven— and that's exactly what we find in the Bible.

These eight studies will help you develop a biblical view of heaven. You should be warned that the truth you discover might change your present perspective. You might begin to see heaven as a place of limitless possibilities! Our future home is not simply a place separated *from* the evil and pain and sorrow of this world. Heaven is also an entrance *into* incredible joy, peace, activity, responsibility and rest.

We will be exploring some aspects of our future life that don't usually come to mind when we think about heaven but they are all part of the Bible's perspective on the joyful future God has prepared for us. The studies are not focused only on the future, however. We will also examine how a biblical perspective on heaven changes the way we live today.

This study guide may challenge some views about heaven that you've held a long time. But don't despair. The old views will be replaced by truths that are fuller, richer and more exciting than anything you've even imagined before.

Suggestions for Individual Study

1. As you begin each study, pray that God will speak to you through his Word.

2. Read the introduction to the study and respond to the personal reflection question or exercise. This is designed to help you focus on God and on the theme of the study.

3. Each study deals with a particular passage—so that you can delve into the author's meaning in that context. Read and reread the passage to be studied. If you are studying a book, it will be helpful to read through the entire book prior to the first study. The questions are written using the language of the New International Version, so you may wish to use that version of the Bible. The New Revised Standard Version is also recommended.

4. This is an inductive Bible study, designed to help you discover for yourself what Scripture is saying. The study includes three types of questions. *Observation* questions ask about the basic facts: who, what, when, where and how. *Interpretation* questions delve into the meaning of the passage. *Application* questions help you discover the implications of the text for growing in Christ. These three keys unlock the treasures of Scripture.

Write your answers to the questions in the spaces provided or in a personal journal. Writing can bring clarity and deeper understanding of yourself and of God's Word.

5. It might be good to have a Bible dictionary handy. Use it to look up any unfamiliar words, names or places.

6. Use the prayer suggestion to guide you in thanking God for what you have learned and to pray about the applications that have come to mind.

7. You may want to go on to the suggestion under "Now or Later," or you may want to use that idea for your next study.

Suggestions for Members of a Group Study

1. Come to the study prepared. Follow the suggestions for individual study mentioned above. You will find that careful preparation will greatly enrich your time spent in group discussion.

2. Be willing to participate in the discussion. The leader of your group will not be lecturing. Instead, he or she will be encouraging the members of the group to discuss what they have learned. The leader will be asking the questions that are found in this guide.

3. Stick to the topic being discussed. Your answers should be based on the verses which are the focus of the discussion and not on outside authorities such as commentaries or speakers. These studies focus on a particular passage of Scripture. Only rarely should you refer to other portions of the Bible. This allows for everyone to participate in in-depth study on equal ground.

4. Be sensitive to the other members of the group. Listen attentively when they describe what they have learned. You may be surprised by their insights! Each question assumes a variety of answers. Many questions do not have "right" answers, particularly questions that aim at meaning or application. Instead the questions push us to explore the passage more thoroughly.

When possible, link what you say to the comments of others. Also, be affirming whenever you can. This will encourage some of the more hesitant members of the group to participate.

5. Be careful not to dominate the discussion. We are sometimes so eager to express our thoughts that we leave too little opportunity for others to respond. By all means participate! But allow others to also.

6. Expect God to teach you through the passage being discussed and through the other members of the group. Pray that you will have an enjoyable and profitable time together, but also that as a result of the study you will find ways that you can take action individually and/or as a group.

7. Remember that anything said in the group is considered confidential and should not be discussed outside the group unless specific permission is given to do so.

8. If you are the group leader, you will find additional suggestions at the back of the guide.

1

Preparing A Place

My friend in the hospital bed didn't have long to live. Her breathing came in ragged gasps. "I think I saw heaven last night," she whispered. "I saw the lights of the city—and it looked like home."

Home for a follower of Jesus Christ is a place we've never been. It's a place of beauty and rest and wholeness. It's the place where Jesus is.

GROUP DISCUSSION. What is your favorite room in your home or your parent's home? What do you like about it?

PERSONAL REFLECTION. In what specific place do you feel most secure? Where do you feel closest to God?

In the hours before his death Jesus tried to prepare his closest friends for the coming crisis. Two facts were clear: he would be leaving them and they couldn't come with him. But while they were separated, Jesus would be busy—busy preparing a place for their reunion. *Read John 14:1-9.*

1. What tone of voice do you think Jesus used in verses 1-4?

Did his tone change when he responded to the questions from Thomas (v. 5) and Philip (v. 8)? Explain your answer.

2. What facts about heaven does Jesus relate to his disciples?

3. Why would Jesus' absence produce troubled hearts in his disciples?

4. What troubles your heart?

Who or what do you turn to or rely on when you are upset?

_____

5. What does Jesus have to do to "prepare" the Father's house for us?

_____

6. In what ways is Jesus preparing you to go to the Father's house?

_____

7. What do you expect to see and do in the Father's house?

_____

8. In light of verse 6, how would you respond to a person who believes that any sincere religious belief leads to heaven?

_____

9. Philip thought that if he could just "see" God, all his questions and doubts would disappear. What was Jesus' response (v. 9)?

10. Why did Jesus' promise to return and take the disciples to be with him bring comfort to them?

How does it make you feel knowing that Jesus has promised to return?

Give your troubles to God and then wait for his comfort to calm your heart.

Now or Later

Think of someone who is going through a crisis or difficult time. How do Jesus' words in John 14 equip you to bring comfort or encouragement to that person? Write a letter or talk to the person about what you have learned from this passage. Commit yourself to pray for that person's need.

2

The Last Frontier

I am about to celebrate my fiftieth birthday. (Gulp!) An aging population, loud voices promoting assisted suicide, skyrocketing health care costs and widely publicized near-death experiences have made us a society more and more anxious about death.

What we want to know is—what happens after we die? A lot of people will tell you what they *think* will happen or what they *heard* had happened to someone else, but that's not enough for me. When I stand beside a fresh grave or face that final passage myself, I want more than someone's experience or speculation to hold on to. I want truth. The only reliable source of information about death and what comes after is the Bible. That's because only one reliable witness has passed through death and come back to tell us about it. His name is Jesus.

GROUP DISCUSSION. What accounts of near-death or after-death experiences have you heard or read? What has been your response to those accounts?

PERSONAL REFLECTION. Consider how long you think your life will be. Ask God to use this study to prepare you to face life *and* death with confidence.

The apostle Paul found himself pulled in two directions. On one hand he wanted to live on so he could continue his work of proclaiming the gospel and nurturing new Christians. But another desire tugged at his heart too. There were days when he wanted to untie the rope of this life and set sail for heaven's shore. *Read Philippians 1:19-30.*

1. Paul wrote this letter when he was under arrest in Rome, waiting for a trial before the Roman emperor. How would you describe Paul's attitude in these verses?

2. What would your attitude be in circumstances similar to Paul's?

3. Do most people today think that death brings "gain" (v. 21)? Explain your answer.

4. What responsibilities kept Paul linked to this life (vv. 22, 25-26)?

5. What were his expectations about being with Christ (v. 23)?

6. The word *depart* (v. 23) was used in Paul's day to picture a ship being untied from the dock and setting sail for a new destination. If you view death in that light, does it make death a more positive experience or a more uncertain one? Why?

7. Paul seemed so certain about what would happen at death. What was his sense of security based on?

8. Do you feel the same assurance when you think about your own death? Why or why not?

9. What spiritual legacy did Paul want to leave in the lives of these Christians (vv. 27-30)?

10. What legacy do you want to leave in the lives of your family members?

your friends?

11. What can you do to strengthen the positive impact you are having on those around you?

Thank Jesus for dying in your place and for removing death's painful sting.

Now or Later

The Bible uses several images to picture death. Read these passages and consider whether your view of death accurately (or inaccurately) mirrors the biblical view of death. Death is pictured as:

☐ *Sleep*—because it is temporary and ends in a great awakening (1 Corinthians 15:51)

☐ *An exodus*—as joyful release from bondage (Luke 9:31; 2 Peter 1:14-15)

☐ *Taking down a tent*—our earthly body dies but we receive a new, glorified body (2 Corinthians 5:1, 4)

☐ *Coming home*—we go to a place of rest and security (2 Corinthians 5:6-8)

For people without the assurance of salvation and forgiveness in Christ, the Bible pictures death as a "terror" (Psalm 55:4) and an "enemy" (1 Corinthians 15:25-26).

3

Rapture Ahead!

1 Thessalonians 4:13-18

Most of us think of heaven as a place we go to after death. But one generation of Christians won't experience death! When Jesus returns to take his followers to heaven, those of us who are alive at that moment will be changed forever.

GROUP DISCUSSION. What will happen when Jesus returns? On a small card or piece of paper, each member of the group should write one thing he or she has heard or has thought will happen at the time of Christ's return. As the leader reads each response, talk about whether or not you think that particular event will really happen or not.

PERSONAL REFLECTION. What feelings come to mind when you think about Christ's return? Ask the Lord to use this study to encourage you to look forward to that moment with anticipation and joy.

Paul's teaching about Jesus' return was prompted by a problem in the Thessalonian church. These Christians were concerned about fellow believers who had died. When Paul was with them, he had told them about Jesus' return to take believers to heaven. But after Paul left, some of the Christians had died. Would they miss Christ's coming? Would their bodies be left behind? Would these Christians ever see their friends again? *Read 1 Thessalonians 4:13-18.*

---

1. As you glance through the passage again, do you think Paul looked toward Christ's return with anticipation or with dread? What specific words or statements in the passage lead you to that conclusion?

---

2. Why is a Christian's grief over the death of a friend different than the grief of the person who doesn't have a relationship with Christ (vv. 13-14)?

---

3. What was the source of Paul's teaching about Christ's return (v. 15), and why is that important?

---

4. What sequence of events does Paul lay out (vv. 16-17)?

5. Do you think everyone in the world will hear the shout, the angel's voice and the trumpet blast (v. 16) or just the Christians? Explain your answer.

6. Paul included himself among those who would still be alive at Jesus' coming ("*we* who are still alive," v. 17). What does that tell you about when Paul expected Jesus to come back?

7. If you knew for certain that Jesus would return in one week, how would your life change?

Who would you seek out to talk to about believing in Jesus as Savior and Lord?

8. Do you think Paul's instruction calmed the concerns of the Thessalonian Christians or did it just raise more questions? Explain.

9. What effect did Paul want his teaching to have on Christians (v. 18)?

How did this passage have that effect on you?

_____

10. What confident hope can you share from this passage with someone who is convinced that death is the end of our existence?

Give God praise for the assurance he gives us of being "with the Lord forever."

Now or Later

In 1 Corinthians 15 Paul gives us more instruction about what will happen to us when Jesus returns. *Read 1 Corinthians 15:51-54.* What additional insight about Christ's return for Christians does this passage give you?

Read 15:58 for some practical ways this teaching will change your life.

4

Run
to Win

I am convinced that if the apostle Paul were on earth today, he would be an avid sports fan. Paul saw powerful parallels between the discipline needed for athletic competition and the endurance required to live the Christian life. Both endeavors call for an intense, single-minded focus on winning. Both demand hard work and rigorous training. At the end of the Christian race here on earth just like at the end of an athletic event, those who have run with endurance receive a reward.

GROUP DISCUSSION. Describe an award or recognition you have received at some time in your life. If you have a trophy or certificate, show it to the group.

PERSONAL REFLECTION. Would you describe yourself as a competitive person? Why or why not?

Part of our entrance into heaven will be an evaluation of our lives by Jesus himself. The Bible tells us that as followers of Christ, we will give an account of our lives to Jesus (2 Corinthians 5:10; Romans 14:10-12). Jesus' evaluation of us will not be to see if we are saved or lost. That issue was settled when we believed on Jesus and received eternal life by his grace alone. The evaluation we will face will be an evaluation of what we did in life with the gifts and opportunities God gave us. The results of that evaluation will bring us either reward or loss of reward. *Read 1 Corinthians 9:24-27.*

---

1. What individual sports or aspects of athletic training and competition does Paul refer to in these verses?

---

2. Are you comfortable comparing the Christian life with athletic competition? Why or why not?

---

3. What "prize" (v. 24) and "crown" (v. 25) did Paul want to receive?

4. Think about what motivates you to serve the Lord in some area of ministry. Are you doing it to receive a reward or for some other reason?

5. What disciplines are essential to become a world-class athlete?

What spiritual disciplines are part of the "strict training" (v. 25) to become an effective, mature Christian?

6. Which of these spiritual disciplines is most well-developed in your life and which is least?

7. What might disqualify a believer from receiving the prize for serving the Lord (v. 27)?

8. How would you describe your place in the Christian race right now: on the sidelines? ready to quit? going great?

9. What do you need from the Lord or from others to help you keep running strong?

10. How does the promise of heaven as you are coming to understand it encourage you to stay in the race?

Ask God to give you the focus and dedication you need to faithfully serve him.

Now or Later

Carve out some quiet time to realistically evaluate your Christian commitment and obedience to Jesus Christ. If you gave an account of your life to Jesus today, which aspects would you be confident in and which would bring you shame?

5

Practicing Our Praise

Revelation 4

Christians are rediscovering the importance of worship. For a long time we've had a very weak view of worship. We thought that worship was something done *for* us by the people in front of the church. But in the Bible we find that worship is active. Worship is something done *by* us as individual believers and as part of a believing community. Worship is our declaration of God's supreme worth. In genuine worship, God is the audience and we are the worshipers. Our goal is to exalt and honor God alone.

GROUP DISCUSSION. What elements make up a typical church worship service? In light of the opening paragraph, decide which elements are most effective in prompting genuine worship and which are least effective. Then discuss how we as believers can more actively participate in each part of the service.

PERSONAL REFLECTION. How do you best express your love and adoration to God—in music, prayer, giving, ministry or compassion to others?

Begin this study by expressing praise to God for the greatness of his character and the goodness of his blessings to you.

When the Bible allows us to look into heaven, we usually see a scene of worship. One of the most dramatic scenes is in Revelation 4. God is in the center of everything and the inhabitants of heaven give him joyful praise. *Read Revelation 4.*

---

1. Imagine yourself as a CNN reporter covering this scene. What images would you want the camera to capture?

What sounds would you want your audience to hear?

What emotions would you want people watching to experience?

---

2. Who is the one seated on the throne and what impresses you about him?

---

3. Who are the twenty-four elders and what is communicated by the way they are dressed (v. 4)?

4. The "four living creatures" (vv. 6-8) are (apparently) angels who surround the throne of God. How are the four beings similar to each other and how are they different?

—————————————————————————————

5. What aspects of God's character do these living creatures exalt, and why do they focus on those specific qualities (v. 8)?

What aspects of God's character do you tend to focus on when you worship him? Why?

—————————————————————————————

6. Worship will be one of our main activities in heaven. Does that fact heighten your anticipation of heaven or diminish it? Explain your answer.

—————————————————————————————

7. How would you respond to someone who thinks heaven will just be one, eternal, boring church service?

8. What attitudes toward God are expressed by the elders in verses 10-11?

In what specific ways can we express those same attitudes in our worship today?

---

9. What would this vision of worship in heaven have communicated to the persecuted Christians who first read it?

What does it say to us when we feel like our world is out of control?

Pray Revelation 4:11 as your own declaration of God's worth.

Now or Later

Revelation 5 continues the scene of worship in heaven but attention is focused on Jesus, the Lamb of God. Read through the chapter. Then compose your own expression of one of the "praise songs" (vv. 9-10, 12, 13). Your personal expression of adoration might be a poem, prayer, sketch or painting of this incredible scene, or it might be a song. Use it to give praise and honor to God and to his Son, Jesus Christ.

6

Welcome to the Party!

I should have known from the name of the restaurant that I wasn't dressed appropriately. The light in my brain only turned on, however, when I stepped out of the elevator and saw my date's father in a three-piece suit. My girlfriend had invited me to dinner so her parents could meet me—and I made quite an impression. The headwaiter found a wrinkled sport coat for me to put on over my sweater and jeans. The meal conversation was cordial enough, but the break-up over the phone the next day was anything but friendly. This girl I liked so well didn't want to hitch her wagon to such a social clod.

GROUP DISCUSSION. Describe an experience in which you felt out of place socially (or a situation you imagine would make you feel out of place).

PERSONAL REFLECTION. What kind of people are you most uncomfortable with?

What kind of people was Jesus most uncomfortable with?

Jesus shocked a group of very religious people one day when he began talking about those who would sit down at the great feast inaugurating God's kingdom. Some men and women who never imagined they would get a glimpse of that feast would find themselves seated as honored guests—and some who were certain they had earned a place at the table by their pious works would be excluded from the banquet hall. *Read Luke 14:7-24.*

1. Put yourself at this dinner party with Jesus. What different emotions would you as a guest (or as the host) have felt as Jesus told the three parables (vv. 7-11, 12-14, 15-24)?

2. How did Jesus' view of honor and prestige differ from the views held by others attending the dinner (vv. 7-11)?

3. If you were to give a banquet for "the poor, the crippled, the lame, the blind" (v. 13), who would you invite?

How does Jesus say you will be rewarded (v. 14)?

4. When Jesus returns from heaven, earthly kingdoms will be replaced by God's kingdom. That future kingdom is often pictured in the Bible as a great banquet. What does that tell you about the spirit and attitude that will characterize the kingdom age?

5. Did the person who spoke in verse 15 want to affirm what Jesus had said in the previous verses, or did he have a different goal in mind? Explain your answer.

6. The three guests invited to the banquet in Jesus' parable had been informed in advance that the banquet would be held. The servant who called them was simply telling them the banquet was ready. In that light, what do you think of the excuses the three guests gave (vv. 18-20)?

7. Jesus is talking in the parable about God's invitation to participate in his future kingdom. Who are "the poor, the crippled, the blind and the lame" (v. 21) the servant is commanded to invite?

Who are those he urges to come in from the roads and country lanes (v. 23)?

8. Why will none of those originally invited get a taste of God's "banquet" (v. 24)?

9. How does your responsibility as a Christian parallel the servant's role in the parable?

10. What kinds of people should you invite to God's banquet?

11. Many Christians picture themselves in heaven surrounded by people of the same ethnic background, economic status and denominational conviction. What specific steps can you take to broaden your perspective toward those who will be part of God's kingdom?

Thank God for graciously inviting you into his kingdom.

Now or Later

This week take a person to lunch or buy a surprise gift for someone who can't repay you. Love and grace are to be given, not simply exchanged. Look particularly for a person on the fringe of your normal circle of friends. God honors those who have friends on all levels of the social ladder.

7

Working for
Your Father

Matthew 25:14-30

I learned to work from my father. He taught his three children to start a job promptly, stick to the task diligently and finish well—and if we didn't demonstrate enough enthusiasm, he provided some! As much as I grumbled about work in my younger years, I've seen my father's instruction pay multiple rewards as an adult. The habit of faithfully carrying through on small things has opened doors to increasing responsibilities and more satisfying rewards.

GROUP DISCUSSION. Who has made the most significant impact (positive or negative) on how you work? Be prepared to give a demonstration to the group of how that person motivated you—or failed to motivate you.

PERSONAL REFLECTION. What task do you find easiest to put off? What have been the consequences of delay?

In the middle of a long sermon about his future return from heaven to usher in God's kingdom, Jesus told an instructive story or parable about a wealthy man who was leaving on a long journey. Since he wouldn't be able to manage his assets personally, the man entrusted his money to his three servants. His response to each servant's investment strategy will give us new insight into how we are to use what God has entrusted to our care. *Read Matthew 25:14-30.*

1. As you think through this story, what sort of man is the master?

2. What do you think the first two servants did with the money given to them in order to double it?

How did the master respond to their resourcefulness?

3. What do you think of the master's response to the third servant?

4. Why did the third servant hide his money when he knew the master was "a hard man" who would expect a good return (vv. 24-25)?

5. What abilities or resources has God entrusted to you?

6. As you think back through the story, who or what is represented by the wealthy man?

his journey?

the servants?

the talents of money?

7. If the master returned today, what would he say to you about how you have invested the abilities he has placed in your care?

8. If we are faithful with what God has now entrusted to us, how will we be rewarded in the future kingdom (vv. 21, 23)?

9. What will happen if we are like the lazy servant and misuse what God has given us (vv. 28-30)?

10. What one ability or resource can you use this week to communicate Christ's love or to do God's work?

11. What specific step can you take to remind yourself to manage wisely the gifts God has entrusted to you?

Ask God to give you wisdom to see opportunities to serve him with your skills and resources.

Now or Later

If you have the resources, randomly give each member of your group an envelope with money in it ($1.00, $5.00 or $10.00, for example). Challenge them to invest that money in God's kingdom before your next study and be prepared to share with the group any "return" on the investment that they received.

8

Looking for the City

When I was a child, I imagined heaven as a place filled with enormous buildings, inhabited by eerie, white-robed people and patrolled by angelic police! Then my grandparents died, and a dear pastor friend died, and my wife's parents died, and Christian friends I have come to love deeply have died. Now I think of heaven in terms of the people who are there, people I love, people I'm anxious to see again.

GROUP DISCUSSION. What is the most beautiful place you have ever been? Describe the place in terms of sights and sounds.

PERSONAL REFLECTION. How do you envision heaven? What faces of friends who have died are part of the picture?

When a Christian dies, he or she is with the Lord immediately in a place we call *heaven.* As wonderful as that place is, it is only temporary. After the future resurrection of our bodies and the final judgment of God on those who have rejected his grace, God will bring our present universe to an end. Then in a dazzling display of power, God will create a new heaven and new earth as our dwelling place forever. The apostle John caught a glimpse of God's new creation, and words almost failed to describe the glorious sight he saw. *Read Revelation 21—22.*

1. As you look back through these chapters, what one scene would you like to capture in a photograph?

What fact about heaven is new to you?

What promise from God is most significant?

2. What has caused you "mourning or crying or pain" over the past year?

How does it make you feel to know that these old things will pass away (21:4)?

3. Why did God reveal to John so many details about the new Jerusalem—the measurements, the stones, the streets (21:12-21)?

4. What will be missing from the future city (21:22-27), and why is each absence significant?

5. According to 22:1-5, what will the inhabitants of the city be doing?

6. Who is excluded from the city (21:8; 22:15)?

What do their actions on earth demonstrate about their relationship with Jesus Christ?

7. Who can gain entrance to God's city, and on what basis does that person enter (22:17)?

8. What might a person add to or take away from God's words (22:18-19)?

9. In what specific ways can you respect and honor the truth that God has spoken in the book of Revelation (and, by extension, in the whole Bible)?

10. Do you feel more prepared or less prepared for a future in heaven as a result of these studies? Explain why.

Heaven is prepared for those who have made reservations by trusting in Jesus Christ as Savior and Lord in this life. If you have never believed in Jesus, today is your opportunity to accept his gift of forgiveness and eternal life. If you have received Christ, express your gratitude to him for his promise of an eternity in heaven with him.

Now or Later

Develop a worship service based on Revelation 21 and 22. What songs would you sing in that heavenly setting? What would the content of your prayers be? What would the sermon topic be—or would there even be a sermon? Translate your plan into an actual time of praise and thanks to God for the certain hope you have of eternity in his direct presence.

Leader's Notes

MY GRACE IS SUFFICIENT FOR YOU. (2 COR 12:9)

Leading a Bible discussion can be an enjoyable and rewarding experience. But it can also be *scary*—especially if you've never done it before. If this is your feeling, you're in good company. When God asked Moses to lead the Israelites out of Egypt, he replied, "O Lord, please send someone else to do it"! (Ex 4:13). It was the same with Solomon, Jeremiah and Timothy, but God helped these people in spite of their weaknesses, and he will help you as well.

You don't need to be an expert on the Bible or a trained teacher to lead a Bible discussion. The idea behind these inductive studies is that the leader guides group members to discover for themselves what the Bible has to say. This method of learning will allow group members to remember much more of what is said than a lecture would.

These studies are designed to be led easily. As a matter of fact, the flow of questions through the passage from observation to interpretation to application is so natural that you may feel that the studies lead themselves. This study guide is also flexible. You can use it with a variety of groups—student, professional, neighborhood or church groups. Each study takes forty-five to sixty minutes in a group setting.

There are some important facts to know about group dynamics and encouraging discussion. The suggestions listed below should enable you to effectively and enjoyably fulfill your role as leader.

Preparing for the Study

1. Ask God to help you understand and apply the passage in your

own life. Unless this happens, you will not be prepared to lead others. Pray too for the various members of the group. Ask God to open your hearts to the message of his Word and motivate you to action.

2. Read the introduction to the entire guide to get an overview of the entire book and the issues which will be explored.

3. As you begin each study, read and reread the assigned Bible passage to familiarize yourself with it.

4. This study guide is based on the New International Version of the Bible. It will help you and the group if you use this translation as the basis for your study and discussion.

5. Carefully work through each question in the study. Spend time in meditation and reflection as you consider how to respond.

6. Write your thoughts and responses in the space provided in the study guide. This will help you to express your understanding of the passage clearly.

7. It might help to have a Bible dictionary handy. Use it to look up any unfamiliar words, names or places. (For additional help on how to study a passage, see chapter five of *How to Lead a LifeBuilder Study*, IVP, 2018.)

8. Consider how you can apply the Scripture to your life. Remember that the group will follow your lead in responding to the studies. They will not go any deeper than you do.

9. Once you have finished your own study of the passage, familiarize yourself with the leader's notes for the study you are leading. These are designed to help you in several ways. First, they tell you the purpose the study guide author had in mind when writing the study. Take time to think through how the study questions work together to accomplish that purpose. Second, the notes provide you with additional background information or suggestions on group dynamics for various questions. This information can be useful when people have difficulty understanding or answering a question. Third, the leader's notes can alert you to potential problems you may encounter during the study.

10. If you wish to remind yourself of anything mentioned in the leader's notes, make a note to yourself below that question in the study.

Leading the Study

1. Begin the study on time. Open with prayer, asking God to help the group to understand and apply the passage.

2. Be sure that everyone in your group has a study guide. Encourage the group to prepare beforehand for each discussion by reading the introduction to the guide and by working through the questions in the study.

3. At the beginning of your first time together, explain that these studies are meant to be discussions, not lectures. Encourage the members of the group to participate. However, do not put pressure on those who may be hesitant to speak during the first few sessions. You may want to suggest the following guidelines to your group.

☐ Stick to the topic being discussed.

☐ Your responses should be based on the verses which are the focus of the discussion and not on outside authorities such as commentaries or speakers.

☐ These studies focus on a particular passage of Scripture. Only rarely should you refer to other portions of the Bible. This allows for everyone to participate in in-depth study on equal ground.

☐ Anything said in the group is considered confidential and will not be discussed outside the group unless specific permission is given to do so.

☐ We will listen attentively to each other and provide time for each person present to talk.

☐ We will pray for each other.

4. Have a group member read the introduction at the beginning of the discussion.

5. Every session begins with a group discussion question. The question or activity is meant to be used before the passage is read. The question introduces the theme of the study and encourages group members to begin to open up. Encourage as many members as possible to participate, and be ready to get the discussion going with your own response.

This section is designed to reveal where our thoughts or feelings need to be transformed by Scripture. That is why it is especially important not to read the passage before the discussion question is asked. The passage will tend to color the honest reactions people would otherwise give because they are, of course, supposed to think the way the Bible does.

You may want to supplement the group discussion question with an icebreaker to help people to get comfortable. See the community section of the *Small Group Starter Kit* (IVP, 1995) for more ideas.

You also might want to use the personal reflection question with your group. Either allow a time of silence for people to respond individually or discuss it together.

6. Have a group member (or members if the passage is long) read aloud the passage to be studied. Then give people several minutes to read the passage again silently so that they can take it all in.

7. Question 1 will generally be an overview question designed to briefly survey the passage. Encourage the group to look at the whole passage, but try to avoid getting sidetracked by questions or issues that will be addressed later in the study.

8. As you ask the questions, keep in mind that they are designed to be used just as they are written. You may simply read them aloud. Or you may prefer to express them in your own words.

There may be times when it is appropriate to deviate from the study guide. For example, a question may have already been answered. If so, move on to the next question. Or someone may raise an important question not covered in the guide. Take time to discuss it, but try to keep the group from going off on tangents.

9. Avoid answering your own questions. If necessary, repeat or rephrase them until they are clearly understood. Or point out something you read in the leader's notes to clarify the context or meaning. An eager group quickly becomes passive and silent if they think the leader will do most of the talking.

10. Don't be afraid of silence. People may need time to think about the question before formulating their answers.

11. Don't be content with just one answer. Ask, "What do the rest of you think?" or "Anything else?" until several people have given answers to the question.

12. Acknowledge all contributions. Try to be affirming whenever possible. Never reject an answer. If it is clearly off-base, ask, "Which verse led you to that conclusion?" or again, "What do the rest of you think?"

13. Don't expect every answer to be addressed to you, even though this will probably happen at first. As group members become more at ease, they will begin to truly interact with each other. This is one sign of healthy discussion.

14. Don't be afraid of controversy. It can be very stimulating. If you don't resolve an issue completely, don't be frustrated. Move on and keep it in mind for later. A subsequent study may solve the problem.

15. Periodically summarize what the group has said about the passage. This helps to draw together the various ideas mentioned and gives continuity to the study. But don't preach.

16. At the end of the Bible discussion you may want to allow group members a time of quiet to work on an idea under "Now or Later." Then discuss what you experienced. Or you may want to encourage group members to work on these ideas between meetings. Give an opportunity during the session for people to talk about what they are learning.

17. Conclude your time together with conversational prayer, adapting the prayer suggestion at the end of the study to your group. Ask for God's help in following through on the commitments you've made.

18. End on time.

Many more suggestions and helps are found in *How to Lead a LifeBuilder Study.*

Components of Small Groups

A healthy small group should do more than study the Bible. There are four components to consider as you structure your time together.

Nurture. Small groups help us to grow in our knowledge and love of God. Bible study is the key to making this happen and is the foundation of your small group.

Community. Small groups are a great place to develop deep friendships with other Christians. Allow time for informal interaction before and after each study. Plan activities and games that will help you get to know each other. Spend time having fun together—going on a picnic or cooking dinner together.

Worship and prayer. Your study will be enhanced by spending time praising God together in prayer or song. Pray for each other's needs—and keep track of how God is answering prayer in your group. Ask God to help you to apply what you are learning in your study.

Outreach. Reaching out to others can be a practical way of applying what you are learning, and it will keep your group from becoming self-focused. Host a series of evangelistic discussions for your friends or neighbors. Clean up the yard of an elderly friend. Serve at a soup kitchen together, or spend a day working in the community.

Many more suggestions and helps in each of these areas are found in the *Small Group Starter Kit.* You will also find information on building a small group. Reading through the starter kit will be worth your time.

Study 1. Preparing a Place. John 14:1-9.

Purpose: To explore Jesus' promise of his future return and a home forever in heaven.

Group discussion. If you are not familiar with one another's homes, suggest to group members that they bring along a picture of their favorite room to show the group.

Question 2. Jesus emphasizes that he will be reunited with his followers in the future. Whatever else heaven is, we will find our deepest satisfaction in being *with* Christ.

Question 3. The disciples had known Jesus' personal presence for three years. Now it seemed they would be abandoned. In a sense, these men had invested everything in Jesus. They had left businesses and career paths to follow him—and it was all about to evaporate.

Jesus later promised not to abandon them but to send them another comforter who would care for them just as Jesus had (14:17-18).

The disciples would have to trust Jesus' promises even when it appeared that their world was collapsing. Within a few hours, Jesus would be arrested and condemned to die. The disciples would be on the run.

Question 5. Jesus had to first prepare the way into heaven by his death on the cross, his resurrection in victory and his ascension into heaven. His finished work of redemption opened the way for us into the presence of the Father. Jesus is also preparing his people for heaven. We will be presented to Christ as his pure bride (Ephesians 4:25-27).

Question 6. Heaven is not the only "construction project" Jesus is involved in. We are being made like Christ through the experiences of life. The key is to believe that God is at work in our lives even when he seems to be far away or unconcerned.

Question 7. This is a good place for imagination but ultimately what we believe and know about heaven has to be based on what the Bible teaches.

Question 8. Jesus makes it very clear that he is the *only* way to God. You may have members of your group who think that is an elitist claim. The only response is that Jesus himself made the claim. We as Christians simply agree with what Jesus said.

Question 9. Several times in John's Gospel Jesus puts himself on the same level with God the Father. In verse 1 of John 14 Jesus said, "You trust in God; now trust to the same degree in me" (my paraphrase). Then in verse 9 Jesus said that if the disciples had seen him, it was exactly like seeing God the Father. All the fullness of God's nature dwells visibly in Jesus (Col 1:19; 2:9; Heb 1:3). If you want to see God, look at Jesus!

Question 10. Some people may feel frightened or anxious about Jesus' return. Explore the reasons they feel that way. If they have never believed in Jesus as Savior and Lord, this is a good opportunity to present the gospel. If they feel unworthy or unforgiven, you may have to urge them to confess sin in their lives and to live obediently. The promise of Jesus' return should be a source of comfort and assurance *and* a motivation to godly living.

Study 2. The Last Frontier. Philippians 1:19-30.

Purpose: To understand the biblical view of death—and to bring our personal view of death into agreement with the Bible's view.

Group discussion. The goal of this exercise is not to debate every detail of the near-death or after-death experiences that members of the group bring up. Keep close track of the time. The best approach to some of the "stickier" issues these experiences may raise is to say: "Our objective in this study is to examine the *Bible's* view of death. Then later we can compare this person's experience to what the Bible teaches."

Question 1. Philippians is one of Paul's "prison letters." At the end of the book of Acts, Paul is in Rome under house arrest, waiting for a hearing before Nero. After his arrest in Jerusalem, Paul (as a Roman citizen) had appealed to Caesar to determine if the charges brought against him by his fellow Jews were valid. Paul expected to be released from his chains but the possibility certainly existed that he would be condemned and executed.

If you feel comfortable in your group, you could follow this question with one that they may find very convicting: "How would you finish the sentence 'For me to live is _____'?"

Question 4. In spite of extreme hardships, Paul had seen abundant "fruit" in his ministry. Dozens of churches had been established and hundreds of Christians were under his spiritual care. Paul had the assurance that if he continued to live, the fruitful labor would also continue. He was also burdened for the spiritual growth and progress of the Christians who looked to him for leadership.

Question 5. Two phrases in verse 23 summarize Paul's anticipation about life after death. First, he would be "with Christ." Since his relationship to Christ was the primary priority of his existence (v. 21), whatever brought him closer to the Lord was welcomed. Second, life after death then was "better by far" than anything he could experience in this life.

Question 6. There is always anticipation and excitement as we start out on a new journey or adventure. We look forward to the destination and even to the journey that gets us there. What may make the journey through death difficult is that the destination seems uncertain or unknown. For Paul it was enough that he would be "with Christ."

Question 7. Paul does not write these verses simply as expressions of what he *hopes* will happen after death. He writes about life beyond the grave with solid confidence. He based his security on the truth he had received from the Lord.

Question 9. Paul wanted these Christians to pursue spiritual maturity whether Paul was around or not. The promises of the gospel message were not dependent on Paul but on God who had given them.

Questions 10-11. The follow-up question to ask as each person explains what legacy he or she wants to leave behind is "What are you doing right now to develop that legacy?" You may not want to press for an answer, but each person has to examine his or her own life. We *are* leaving a legacy. Is it the one we *want* to leave or not?

Study 3. Rapture Ahead! 1 Thessalonians 4:13-18.
Purpose: To be encouraged by the promise of Christ's return for his followers.

General note. In this passage Paul focuses on Christ's return for his followers. Christians call this event "the rapture." The word *rapture* does not occur anywhere in the Bible as a description of Jesus' second coming. The Greek words translated "caught up" in English (1 Thess 4:17) were translated as *rapturo* in the Latin Bible. It means to be snatched away suddenly and forcibly. *When* the rapture will take place in relation to other end-time events has been the subject of long debate among Christians. What we do agree on is that Jesus *is* coming back and we will be with him forever. The goal of this study is not to debate the timing of the rapture but to explore the confident hope the rapture brings to us.

Group discussion. The purpose of this activity is not to get into a long discussion over each suggestion but simply to come to a general consensus. The goals are to get the group thinking about what will happen at Christ's return and to prompt them to seek reliable answers from Scripture.

Question 2. Christians do grieve when someone dies because of the separation from that person. But our grief is not a hopeless grief. We are confident that we will once again see believers who have died. It is more difficult, of course, when someone dies who has not received Jesus as Savior, but even then we can rest in the fact that all judgment is in God's hands and he will do what is right. The person who does *not* have the hope that Christ gives grieves at death because he or she has no assurance of ever seeing that friend or family member again.

Question 3. Paul gave this instruction from the Lord Jesus himself. This is not simply Paul's opinion or wishful thinking.

Question 4. The Lord will descend with a loud command. The word used here refers to a military command shouted out. Jesus will speak one command and the bodies of all Christians who have died will be raised. (See Jn 5:25; 11:43.) The voice of the archangel will gather the angels of God who play a significant role in the events of the end. The trumpet was used in the Old Testament to assemble God's people before him. The trumpet call will assemble the living believers to a final and permanent gathering before the Lord.

Those who have died as Christians will return with the Lord. Their spirits will be reunited with new resurrected bodies. Christians still alive at the time of Christ's return will not experience death but will immediately be changed (glorified). Both groups will meet the Lord in the air.

Question 6. Paul and the other New Testament writers believed that Jesus could return at any moment. They urged Christians to live in such a way that they were prepared to meet the Lord. See 1 Thessalonians 5:1-11; 1 John 3:2-3; Revelation 22:20.

Question 7. After the members of the group have given their responses to these questions, it might be appropriate to remind them that, since Jesus could return at any moment, they should begin now to prepare themselves to face him. If the Lord is prompting them to speak to another person about believing in Jesus, they should begin to watch for an opportunity and then courageously present their testimony to God's saving power.

Question 10. A person facing death or the death of a friend is often more open to a discussion about eternity than he or she may be at any other time. Sensitivity and genuine concern are important elements to be aware of but a confident presentation of the gospel can be very effective in drawing a person to faith in Christ at a time when the person is already focused on human mortality.

For the next session. Encourage group members to bring an award or trophy with them next time for group "show and tell."

Study 4. Run to Win. 1 Corinthians 9:24-27.

Purpose: To challenge Christians to live in awareness of our future evaluation by Jesus Christ.

Group discussion. Make the response to this activity voluntary in case someone has no award to talk about. Explain that the award could be sports related, but it also could be for honor society membership, musical achievement, a spelling championship or good citizenship—even recognition for perfect attendance!

General note. You may want to read 2 Corinthians 5:10; Romans 14:10-12; and 1 Corinthians 3:10-14 as preparation for this discussion on our future evaluation before Christ. You probably will have to correct some misconceptions among members of the group about that future event. Some Christians have incorrectly looked at this experience as a time of judgment or condemnation, but God's promise is that there is *no* condemnation to those who believe in Christ (Rom 8:1). This future event (sometimes called "the judgment seat of Christ" is more accurately referred to as an evaluation. Christ will reveal our motives as well as our actions, and on the basis of his evaluation we will receive rewards or will lose the rewards we could have received if we had been faithful and obedient to Christ. Christians are not to look toward this event with fear but it *is* a powerful motivation to living in a way that pleases the Lord.

Question 1. Paul draws his imagery from the ancient games held regularly in Corinth and other cities in the Roman Empire. The main event was the foot race in which every athlete competed. They all ran one lap (about 200 yards in Corinth's arena). Paul also refers to boxing (v. 26). The "strict training" (v. 25) was required of every athlete and they all pursued one goal—victory in their chosen event (vv. 24, 27).

Question 2. Some Christians find it very disturbing to apply the imagery of sports competition to the Christian life. Paul's point, however, is not that we are competing against each other in some way. His emphasis is on individual responsibility. Each Christian is challenged to seek to honor the Lord by using his or her abilities and opportunities to serve Christ fully. The arena in which each person operates varies. We have different careers and places of influence. Each person's goal, however, is the same—to hear Christ's commendation.

Question 3. In the athletic games of the ancient world, one victor emerged from each event. The winner was called to stand before the judgment seat, a raised throne at one end of the stadium. A dignitary would then give the winner the prize—a crown, a victor's wreath. The winner was also freed from military duty and taxes for life! The wreath symbolized the culmination of all the discipline of training and effort of winning. Paul is not telling Christians to strive for salvation. We are already accepted in Christ forever. Instead, Paul urges us to seek Christ's approval on all we do *as Christians.*

The book of Revelation pictures Christians in heaven crowned with victor's crowns, rewards for faithful ministry and service to Christ (Rev 4:4). We will lay those crowns back before the throne of God out of gratitude for God's grace and love (Rev 4:10-11).

Question 4. Christians serve the Lord out of love for him, not to earn salvation or to catch God's attention. But Paul also desired to receive Christ's approval on his life. Near the end of his life on earth, Paul was confident that after death he would receive "the crown of righteousness" (2 Tim 4:8). The rewards given to us by Christ will be an indication of our faithfulness to him. They are given to those who run to win.

Question 5. According to Paul, receiving Christ's reward requires diligent effort (v. 24), self-discipline (v. 25) and a focused aim (vv. 26-27). Just as an athlete has a workout routine, the Christian needs exercise in prayer, Bible study, worship, ministry, serving others, meditation, even fasting. Athletes who don't care about winning will do whatever they want. The athletes who care *only* about winning will refuse anything that drags them down.

Question 7. Paul's concern was that after he had called others into the race, he would lose sight of the goal himself and be disqualified. He wasn't talking about losing his eternal standing before God. He was talking about losing his reward. He didn't want to stand before Christ in shame.

Study 5. Practicing Our Praise. Revelation 4.

Purpose: To focus on the worship of God in heaven and the implications for our worship today.

Group discussion. You may want to read the opening paragraph out loud as an introduction to the activity. The activity is not designed to open the door for criticism of a particular church or style of worship. Genuine worship can be expressed regardless of style. Instead discuss the main elements of a typical church service—congregational singing, choir or solo music, announcements, prayer, Scripture reading, sermon, offering, dramatic presentations. Which prompt our active participation? Which don't? Then focus on positive ways to enhance participation in every part of the worship service. Watch your discussion time closely. Depending on the group, this exercise could take your whole study time.

Transition to the Bible study time by singing a worship song (one that focuses on God's character or blessings) or by sharing personal expressions of praise to God.

Question 1. Try to get the group to grasp the overwhelming glory of this scene. All of John's senses were attentive to what was unfolding before him.

Question 2. John does not specifically identify the one on the throne, but the living creatures refer to him as "the Lord God Almighty" (v. 8) and the elders express praise to "our Lord and God" (v. 11). This is obviously God the Father. God the Son, Jesus Christ, comes on the scene in 5:6. God the Holy Spirit is also referred to indirectly in 4:5.

God the Father has no physical body. He is spirit (Jn 4:24) and is not confined by the limitations of a body. John saw the outline or figure of a person, blazing with light.

Question 3. The twenty-four elders represent God's people who are in heaven. Some students of Revelation see them as the church, New Testament believers. Others see both Old Testament Israel and New Testament Christians represented. They are resurrected and robed in purity and are crowned with the victor's crowns of reward.

Question 5. The four living creatures focus primarily on God's holy character. The word *holy* means to be set apart. God is absolutely separate from sin or deceit or error and is totally reserved and committed to good and justice and truth. The four creatures also refer to God's eternity, his faithfulness and his sovereign authority over human affairs ("who was, and is, and is to come," v. 8).

Christians today tend to focus on other aspects of God's character—his love, grace and forgiveness. Every aspect of God's character is perfect and worthy of praise, but the angels who stand continually in his presence point to his holy and pure character as the foundational quality of God's nature.

Question 7. Our worship in heaven will not be hindered by the limitations of our present unredeemed physical bodies and minds. We will not get tired or bored. Our worship of God will be immediate and direct. While worship will be a *primary* activity in heaven, it will not be the *only* activity. We will continually be occupied with new opportunities and challenging responsibilities.

Question 8. Specifically discuss what the elders were demonstrating by falling down before God, by laying their crowns of reward before him and by expressing out loud the worth and majesty of God. Then discuss (part 2) how those same attitudes can be demonstrated in our worship of God today.

Question 9. The Christians this book was written to were under attack because of their faith in Jesus. They needed to be reminded of God's control over his world and over the events in their lives. Ask the members of the group to talk about specific situations in which they may feel like God has abandoned his world or his people.

Study 6. Welcome to the Party! Luke 14:7-24.

Purpose: To acquire Jesus' perspective on what kind of people will be most open to his gracious invitation of salvation.

Question 1. Challenge the group to imagine how they would feel if another guest at a dinner party began to rebuke people for their actions and even embarrassed the host over the matter of what guests the host had invited.

Question 2. As he did often, Jesus turned the normal social customs upside down. People in Jesus' day (just like people today) wanted their position and power recognized and rewarded. Jesus said that true honor comes to the person who is genuinely humble.

Question 3. Jesus was not saying we should never invite our family and friends to a banquet. His point was that our main motive should not be to simply invite people who will invite us back. Instead we need to look at those on the fringes of society or the church or our circle of friends—the people normally overlooked or excluded, the people who would be surprised to receive an invitation from someone like us. Urge the group to think of people beyond the literal "poor, blind and crippled"—to other segments of society who may feel left out. Encourage them to think of practical ways that we can include more of these people in our personal lives and in our church communities.

Question 4. Other passages that picture God's kingdom as a great banquet are Isaiah 25:6-8; Matthew 8:11; 26:29; Revelation 19:9.

Question 5. The remark in verse 15 seems to be a subtle rebuke to Jesus. Everyone was feeling a little uncomfortable, and in a backhanded attempt at breaking the tension, the person said (in effect), "Won't it be great when we all get to heaven and these debates will be left behind!" Jesus used the parable in verses 16-24 to challenge those assumptions. Some who think they are in line for God's kingdom will not be at the banquet table at all.

Question 6. The custom in Jesus' day was to send out an invitation to a banquet well in advance, which a guest could accept or decline. Then on the day of the banquet, a servant was sent to summon the previously invited guests. These three men had already accepted the initial invitation (verse 17—they "had been invited") but when they were summoned, they made excuses. Encourage those in your group to examine the excuses. Were the excuses valid or not? How do they parallel the excuses people give today for rejecting God's gracious invitation to receive salvation?

Question 7. The traditional explanation of the parable is that the religious Jews who rejected Jesus would be excluded from God's kingdom. Their places would be taken by the "outcasts" of Jewish society (those "in the town," v. 21)—the very people who responded so positively to Jesus' message. Then even the Gentiles or non-Jews would be invited in (those out on "the roads and country lanes," verse 23).

Challenge the group members to look for present-day applications of the parable. Who might we consider "outsiders" to God's grace? What people might God shock us by saving?

Question 8. It's possible for very pious and religious people to exclude themselves from God's grace by their proud and arrogant trust in their own goodness.

Question 9. God's banquet is ready, but God has entrusted Christians with the responsibility of calling people into the kingdom through the message of the gospel. Do we invest ourselves in pleading only with those who have already been invited countless times, or should we turn our attention to people we have overlooked or considered unworthy of an invitation? Think how the spirit of the banquet must have changed as all the "outsiders" came pouring in! One of the greatest obstacles to evangelism is that "outsiders" will certainly upset our religious routine.

Question 10. The Bible seems to indicate that some of our personal distinctiveness will continue in heaven. In the book of Revelation, John sees a multitude of people in heaven "from every nation, tribe, people and language" (7:9; see also 5:9). Economic and denominational barriers will be gone but God's incredible creativity in his creation will be reflected in us forever.

Study 7. Working for Your Father. Matthew 25:14-30.

Purpose: To examine the use of our resources today in light of our responsibilities in the future.

General note. In preparation for leading this study, you may want to read Jesus' entire sermon (Mt 24—25). Jesus was clearly talking about events still in the future—his return to earth in glory (21:3, 30-31, 37-39, 42; 25:31-32, 34) and the establishment of God's kingdom.

The theme of reward or blessing for faithfulness also comes up several times in the discourse (24:45-51; 25:1-13, 34-40).

Question 2. The master did not tell his servants how to invest the money. He gave them the freedom to use what he had given them to the best advantage. The first two servants managed the master's resources wisely and gained a good return. God gives us a variety of resources—skills, abilities, gifts, money, time, energy—and he gives us the freedom to invest those resources in service to him as we think best. The master never asked the servants *how* they had invested. He was pleased with their hard work and abundant return.

Question 3. The third servant simply hid the money. He didn't want to face the hard work or risk of investing it. Jesus characterized the servant as "wicked" and "lazy" (v. 26). He wasn't afraid of losing the money in an investment plan; he just didn't want to do the work. The servant could have made some return on the money easily and safely by putting his money in the bank. The master got his money back but nothing more.

Question 5. If you want to make it more pointed, you could ask, Are you a five-talent servant, a two-talent servant or a one-talent servant?

There may be questions about the different amounts of money given. The amount given to each servant was dependent on the master's evaluation of their maturity, wisdom and ability. But there was no difference in the master's commendation. The servant who gained two additional talents received the same words of praise as the servant who gained five. In addition, as the servant used his gifts, he found those gifts expanding. As Christians faithfully use what God has given to us, we will find that we are given even more ability and greater opportunities.

Question 6. This parable is usually interpreted as a picture of Jesus (the master, the wealthy man) going back to heaven (on a journey) but leaving Christians (his servants) behind to faithfully use his resources (the talents) in kingdom work. The talents in the parable were a measure of money. A talent was a certain weight of gold, silver or copper. Even *one* talent was a significant amount of money. Our modern-day use of the word *talent* to refer to a skill or ability is derived from this parable.

Question 8. Those who are diligent in using their skills and resources now for God's glory will find their responsibilities magnified and expanded in God's future kingdom. In a similar parable in Luke 19:11-27, the master said, "Because you have been trustworthy in a very small matter, take charge of ten cities" (Lk 19:17). Faithful Christians will be rewarded by being given ruling responsibility in the future age.

Question 9. Those who have done little with what God has placed under their care will have even those gifts taken away and given to others.

Now or Later. Have people choose the envelopes randomly rather than assigning amounts to different people to avoid offense.

Study 8. Looking for the City. Revelation 21—22.

Purpose: To understand and anticipate the glory and joy of eternity with the Lord.

Question 3. The city was a real place, not just a dream or hallucination. The measurements and precise descriptions were designed to impress John's readers with the immensity and beauty of the new Jerusalem. The city forms a perfect cube (or pyramid) 1,400 miles (12,000 stadia) wide, long and high. The base of the city would cover the eastern United States from Maine to Florida and from the Atlantic Ocean to the Mississippi River.

Question 4. John lists several things that will not be in the new Jerusalem: the sea (21:1) to separate people or nations; the temple (21:22), because the worship of God will be direct and immediate; the sun and the moon (21:23), because the glory of the Lord will illuminate the city; the night (21:25), because we will not require rest or sleep in the same way we do today and because activity will never cease; impurity or deceit (21:27), because sin's presence will be removed. You might also ask the group to think about what other places or institutions will be missing: hospitals, funeral homes or cemeteries, prisons, places of sexual or financial exploitation.

Question 5. John says that we will "serve God" (22:3) and "reign for ever and ever" (22:5). Heaven will obviously be a place of activity and responsibility. It might be interesting to ask the group what they envision themselves doing or learning or experiencing in heaven.

If we will be serving God in eternity, it seems reasonable to expect that we will be involved in specific ministry for the Lord now. When we think of "reigning," we need to remember that the greatest in God's kingdom is the one who is the servant of all, the one who uses his or her spiritual gifts to build up the body of Christ.

Question 6. The Bible is not teaching good-works salvation here. We all stumble even as believers in Christ. Those excluded from the future city *practice* these evil deeds and demonstrate by their unrepentant lifestyle that they do not have a faith relationship with Christ.

Question 7. God invites all who are willing to receive his free gift to enter his kingdom. This might be a good time to encourage any in the group who have not made a commitment to Christ to accept his offer of forgiveness and eternal life.

Question 8. These verses refer directly to the book of Revelation but can be applied to all of God's truth. We can add to God's words by developing a list of Christian rules or traditions that go beyond the commands of Scripture—or by following another book or religious leader more closely than we follow the Bible. We can take away from God's words simply by deliberately choosing *not* to obey what Scripture clearly teaches.

On the other hand, Christians show respect and honor for God's words by reading the Bible, memorizing it, meditating on it and most clearly by obeying it.

Douglas Connelly (MDiv and MTh, Grace Theological Seminary) is the senior pastor at Davison Missionary Church, near Flint, Michigan. He is also the author of Angels Around Us *(InterVarsity Press) and* The Bible for Blockheads *(Zondervan), as well as nineteen LifeBuilder Bible Studies.*